# What Music Means to Me

The power of music for people living with dementia

# *What Music Means to Me*

## The power of music for people living with dementia

**CATHERINE SAHADEVAN**

*StoryTerrace*

**Text** Joanna Bawa, on behalf of StoryTerrace

First print June 2025

www.StoryTerrace.com

*Foreword*
*This book is a heart warming memoir that celebrates a tale of success and the spirit of giving it a go. Cathy's book follows her story, and what led her to set up the One Voice Choir at the care home. It's an inspirational tale that shows the joy that music can bring to the hearts and minds of people living with dementia. I was lucky enough to meet Cathy at the Power of Music Report Launch in 2022. She has a warmth that lifts you up like your favourite song. I wish her all the best with this book and the One Voice Choir.*

*Tony Christy*

# CONTENTS

# CHAPTER 1: ROOTS AND EARLY LIFE

Music reaches inside me, pulling out feelings and memories long forgotten. It takes me to places I used to go, reminding me of people I used to know. This powerful connection has been part of me for as long as I can remember.

I was born in Dublin, the youngest of six children, one brother and four sisters. Growing up in 1980s Ireland shaped me profoundly. We lived simpler lives then, where a single record played over and over could become the soundtrack to an entire summer. We didn't have today's technology, so music became our happy place.

Curiously, music wasn't a family tradition. I'm out there on my own. I tell people who ask if I came from a musical household, No, none of my siblings shared my passion, and I sometimes wonder where this love originated from.

I've never been formally trained in music. I tried playing instruments but wasn't very good at it. Instead, I discovered something more powerful: how music made me feel. This connection lived in the emotions a song could stir, the memories it awakened.

At seventeen, I left Dublin for England, carrying little except determination and my love for music. Those songs from home became precious connections to the family and place I'd left behind. This transition built resilience and openness to new experiences that would serve me well.

In England, my life expanded in unexpected ways. I married a Sri Lankan man, hence my surname, Sahadevan, and we had two children. My husband isn't particularly musical; he likes Bob Marley and stuff, but our home was always filled with sound. My children grew up watching my enthusiasm for life, often saying, 'Mum's always doing something. Mum's always trying something new.'

This creativity isn't limited to music. I'm quite a creative person; I can write the odd poem, and I'm quite creative at making things. This natural inclination to create has been a constant throughout my life.

As an adult, I joined a choir. To hear the harmonies from individual voices resonated deeply with me, eventually inspiring work that would touch countless lives.

What I've always understood about music is its extraordinary emotional power. When I hear Love Is All Around, I'm instantly transported to my wedding day. Other songs take me to holidays or significant moments. Music is a feeling, as I wrote in a poem. I don't know why, but sometimes it makes me want to cry. But I soon cheer up because music always lifts my spirits.

When I'm cleaning at home with music turned up loud, I'm just giving it welly singing like I'm on top of the pops. In those moments, I'm completely free, completely myself. That authentic joy radiates outward and touches everyone around me.

I like to make other people happy. I like to make other people laugh, I like to be infectious to other people. This quality would eventually become central to my work.

Before working with the elderly, I studied childcare and spent time caring for children. Both experiences taught me about vulnerability and the need for compassion and creativity in caregiving. They prepared me for a path that would bring together my passion for music and my commitment to enhancing others lives.

I couldn't have predicted how these threads would weave together my Irish roots, my love of music, my creative spirit, and my desire to spread joy. Looking back, each experience prepared me for what was to come.

Music has always been more than entertainment for me, it's been a lifeline, a way of processing emotions, a source of connection. I believe with my whole heart that music reaches more parts of the brain than anything else. It breaks through barriers that words alone cannot penetrate. It speaks directly to the soul.

This understanding would eventually lead me to revelations about dementia, connection, and what remains when memory fades. But first, I needed to find my place in the world of care, to discover how my gifts could make a difference.

# CHAPTER 2: ENTERING THE
# CARE WORLD

Fifteen years ago, I walked through the doors of the care home with no formal qualifications and no real idea what I was getting myself into. I had worked with children before, but caring for the elderly was an entirely different proposition. I remember feeling a mix of nervousness and determination, qualities that would serve me well in the years to come.

Since working in the care industry, I often tell people: I started as a carer, then a care team leader, and nearly seven years ago, I started doing the activities. This simple summary hardly captures the profound journey I've been on, a journey that would transform not just my career but my understanding of humanity itself.

When I first arrived at the care home, dementia was largely a mystery to me. I don't think I'd ever met anybody who had dementia when I first started to work there. I didn't know what it was. I didn't understand it.

The reality of dementia hit me in those early days  its complexity, its unpredictability, the way it manifests so differently in each person. It's so complex, because there's no two people the same.  This wasn't something I could learn from a textbook I had to immerse myself in it, day by day, interaction by interaction.

In those first years, I focused on mastering the basics of care. I earned my care certificate and completed all the mandatory courses the care home offered. The hands-on experience proved invaluable, teaching me things no classroom ever could. I learned to read the subtle signs of distress, to communicate when words failed, to provide comfort in moments of confusion. As I grew more confident, I was promoted to care team leader.

Then came the moment that would unexpectedly change the course of my career. My manager approached me about taking on the Activities Coordinator role. My immediate response absolutely not!

I laugh now, remembering my resistance. It just looked to be such a hard job. You have to be upbeat and creative; you've got to be all these things and more. The responsibility seemed overwhelming, not just organizing activities, but being the person who brought energy, enthusiasm, enjoyment, and engagement every single day.

After some persuasion, I agreed to a compromise. I'll give it a six-week trial. And if I don't like it, I want my other job back. My manager agreed, and somewhat reluctantly, I stepped into this new role, not realising it would become the perfect outlet for talents I didn't even know I possessed.

Those first weeks were challenging. I was learning how to engage people at various stages of dementia, how to create activities that were stimulating but not overwhelming, how to judge when someone needed encouragement and when they needed space. But something unexpected happened, I discovered I had a natural ability for this work.

It's brought the creativity out in me. The activities role unlocked something that had perhaps always been there, waiting for the right opportunity. I found myself coming up with innovative ideas, designing new programs, finding ways to bring joy into the everyday lives of our residents.

The transformation wasn't just in what I did but in who I became. Before I did this, if I had to speak in public, if you put a microphone in my hand, I probably, would, faint or something. Now I confidently address groups, lead performances, speak at events. The nervous woman who once shied away from attention has been replaced by someone who can command a room, who can inspire both residents and staff.

Working with people with dementia requires shedding inhibitions. You can't be self-conscious or worried about looking silly. I burst into the lounge in full song and dance first thing in the morning. laughing at how this would have horrified my former self. But I've learned that this uninhibited enthusiasm is precisely what makes connections possible. You can't have inhibitions, and the residents love that, and that's infectious to them. They're like, 'Woo! What are we doing?'

This energy became my trademark. Even activities that might seem mundane can become exciting with the right approach. 'We're gonna have a game of bingo today.' And what does bingo mean? Prizes!' It's about creating anticipation, generating enthusiasm, and making each day feel special.

Perhaps the most important skill I've developed is adaptability. For some people it means having a quiet conversation. Some people are a little bit more chatty. Some people like a bit more, banter. So you have to adjust yourself according to who you're talking to. Each resident is unique, with their own communication style, their own triggers, their own ways of connecting. Learning to read these differences and respond appropriately has been essential.

I also discovered something fundamental about my work ethic I follow through. If I say I'm gonna do something, I do it. The residents and their families know they can count on me, that I won't promise what I can't deliver. And when I commit to something, I give it my all. If we're gonna do something and it's all bells and whistles, it's gonna be all bells and whistles. There's no half measures.

Structure became important in my approach to activities. I found that residents responded well to knowing what to expect, to having a clear schedule of events to look forward to. This predictability provides security in a world that can often feel confusing and uncertain. It gives shape to days that might otherwise blend together.

Through my work, I've come to understand dementia not as something to fear but as a different way of experiencing the world. It's a stage. It's the next stage of your life. It is not boohoo, doom and gloom, this is the end. It's a different stage of your life. This perspective shift has been crucial  seeing beyond the diagnosis to the person who remains, with all their history, personality, and potential for joy.

One of the unexpected aspects of my role has been building relationships with families. Entering a care home can be a daunting experience for relatives, fraught with guilt, uncertainty, and grief for what's been lost. I found that activities provided a bridge. If you come into a care home, for the family, it can be a very daunting experience. But the music and doing things with the music gives the family something to focus on.

Instead of awkward visits filled with strained conversation, families can participate in activities alongside their loved ones, creating new memories and connections. So they're not just coming in and just, you know, sitting with no conversation. I'm going to see my mother, and that's it. Activities give them shared experiences, talking points, reasons to look forward to visits, and plenty of conversation starters.

As the months passed, my six-week trial extended indefinitely. The activities role ceased to be just a job and became something closer to a calling. I saw firsthand how engagement, creativity, and connection could transform lives not just for the residents but for their families and for the staff who cared for them.

Working with people with dementia has taught me patience, resilience, and creativity. It's challenged me to think differently about communication, about memory, about what makes a life meaningful. Most importantly, it's taught me to live in the moment to recognise that even when a memory fades, the feeling remains.

I never imagined, stepping into the care home all those years ago, that I would find my purpose here. I couldn't have predicted how caring for others would help me discover parts of myself I never knew existed. But that's the beautiful unpredictability of life, sometimes the path you resist most strongly is precisely the one you were meant to walk all along.

The Activities Coordinator role opened a door, but it was music that would eventually lead me through it into a world of connection and possibility I could never have imagined. The choir was waiting just around the corner, ready to transform not just my career but my understanding of what's possible when human hearts connect through song. But first, I had to recognise the unique power of music to reach places nothing else could touch. A realisation that would spark a revolution in how I approached my work.

# CHAPTER 3: THE BIRTH OF ONE VOICE CHOIR

It began with a conversation, one of those seemingly ordinary exchanges that unexpectedly alter the course of your life. Nearly seven years ago, while finding my footing as activities coordinator, I mentioned to a resident that I had once been in a choir myself.

I thought that maybe I could transfer my experiences to the residents, in a different way, I told him.

His eyes lit up. That's a fantastic idea, he responded with such conviction that a spark ignited within me, one that would ultimately transform countless lives.

What compelled me to suggest forming a choir. Not ambition or some grand performance vision, but something far more fundamental. I know how music makes me feel and what it does for me. So I wanted to share that with the residents and for them to have that experience.

I had no formal music training, just a love for music, for all types of music, and an intuitive understanding that music could reach people when conversation couldn't.

Our first song was Heart of My Heart, recommended by a resident so excited she immediately began writing out all the lyrics she could remember for me. Her enthusiasm inspired our approach: creating large-print lyric sheets with highlighted choruses to help residents follow along.

We started small about half a dozen residents, many protesting, Oh, no. I can't sing. We needed a motto to overcome this resistance. If you can talk, you can sing. This simple phrase became permission for people who had perhaps spent decades believing they weren't musical enough.

Creating a safe, welcoming atmosphere proved essential. One gentleman was particularly reluctant, sitting by the door during sessions.

Eventually, his confidence built, and his transformation was remarkable. Within weeks, we went on to do shows with him, and he was like the star of the show. From doorway observer to center stage performer, his journey exemplified what our choir could offer.

I quickly learned that each person with dementia receives music differently. Some people might receive it where they will sing along to a song, which is great. Some other people might receive the music by tapping along or dancing. Understanding these differences was crucial, there was no one-size-fits-all approach.

The early days weren't easy. I'd say it was really hard work at first, I admit there were challenges. Sometimes we'd have people falling asleep, people yawning. But persistence paid off. After a while, they got more and more engaged with the choir, because we all got enthusiastic about it as a group.

To keep everyone's attention, I developed my own sign language to communicate during songs using gestures for louder, bring it down, don't sing, get ready. These visual cues allowed me to direct without interrupting the flow of music.

I learned to break songs into manageable segments. We're not going to just learn a whole song all at once. We would often begin by reading through the lyrics like a story, understanding the narrative before singing. So we might only learn one verse and one chorus in a session. So it's not too much. It's not too overwhelming.

While we initially focused on familiar songs, something remarkable happened as time passed. As we've gone on in time, we're learning songs that they've never heard before, and they're remembering those songs. This capacity to learn new material challenged assumptions about what people with dementia could achieve.

Establishing a consistent routine proved vital. Our choir meetings became structured events with warm-ups, discussions about song choices, and focused practice. This predictability provided security in a world that often felt chaotic for residents with dementia.

A remarkable culture developed around our sessions: If you come into the room, you've got to join in. That's the rule. This applied to everyone, staff, family visitors, and even inspectors! This inclusivity broke down barriers, creating shared experiences that transcended traditional roles.

As weeks turned into months, the choir became more than an activity it became a community. Residents formed friendships through their shared experience. When we're in choir, we are a choir. We're not a group of people in the care home. We're a working choir.

This identity shift was transformative. No longer defined primarily by their diagnosis, choir members became musicians with a purpose. They looked forward to rehearsals and performances. They discussed songs even when I wasn't present. The choir had become part of the fabric of their lives.

I witnessed residents reclaiming skills that dementia had seemed to take from them: reading lyrics, remembering words, and engaging socially. Perhaps most importantly, I refused to patronise them. When performances weren't good enough, I would tell them so with humour and kindness, but with honesty. If it's rubbish, it's rubbish. We're gonna do it again, and they love that.

This approach dignified them as capable individuals rather than patients to be pitied. And the results speak for themselves. The second time they go for the song, my god, the difference.

What began as a conversation with one resident had blossomed into something none of us could have predicted. We weren't just singing together, we were creating a community where music bridged the gaps dementia had created, where abilities were celebrated rather than deficits mourned.

The One Voice Choir had found its voice, and though we were just beginning, the harmony we created together was already transforming lives, note by beautiful note.

# CHAPTER 4: BEYOND THE CARE HOME WALLS

The walls of a care home can sometimes feel like boundaries, invisible lines separating those inside from the wider world. But music has a way of dissolving barriers, creating doorways where once there were only walls. As our choir found its voice, I began dreaming of taking our songs beyond the care home, showing the world what our residents could achieve.

This expansion required a transformation from an informal singing group to something more structured. We have uniforms that we wear. So everybody's the same. We're all professionals. This simple step changed how our residents saw themselves. No longer just care home residents, they became performers, members of a proper choir. On stage, wearing our black and white t-shirts with our distinctive circle logo, we were defined by our music, not our diagnoses.

Taking fourteen to sixteen residents to external venues represents a logistical mountain. The coordination required is immense  from transportation to accessibility, from personal care to emotional support. I approach these excursions with military precision, creating detailed itineraries that both ensure smooth operation and alleviate residents anxiety.

Our first ventures were to neighbouring care homes, bringing music to other residents who might not otherwise experience live performance. These initial successes emboldened us to think bigger.

Every Christmas, we now stage a major production. We hire a hall, and we do a big show where we sell tickets to the community, all friends and family, visitors, staff, everybody. Planning begins far in advance. I'll have already booked the hall a year in advance, with preparations intensifying from September onwards.

In 2023, we reached a milestone that once seemed unimaginable. Through Intergenerational Music Making, we were invited to go to the Royal Albert Hall and perform with schools, care homes, and other care facilities. This wasn't just a performance; it was a meeting of generations, with participants aged between 10 and 95, showcasing the beauty of intergenerational music.

The challenge was significant, learning a completely new song written specifically for the event. Can you imagine? I didn't know the song. They didn't know the song. Nobody knew the song. But you know what we worked on that. We worked at it and we worked at it, and we learned that song.

Standing in the historic Elgar Room, our residents performed alongside children and teenagers, creating a tapestry of voices spanning nearly nine decades of lived experience. Afterward, they gave us a private tour around the Royal Albert Hall as well. The residents were tickled by this special treatment. They thought they were like VIPs.

Another pinnacle moment came when we performed at Universal Music Studios to launch the Power of Music Fund. Before our performance, Tony Christie came to our green room to meet the choir members. This was a very exciting day for us. We then performed to a room full of people from the care world and received a standing ovation.

The contrast between our usual setup and this professional environment was stark. I turned up with my little speaker. And when we got there, we had to go on stage to rehearse, and they had all these technicians and all this malarkey. The sophistication of the equipment, the guy in the booth... microphones... the whole nine yards momentarily intimidated me.

When COVID threatened to isolate us, we adapted rather than retreated. We do a lot of performances on Zoom because we're very up to date now. We even developed our online initiative. Every couple of months, there is a thing that we developed called Musical Memories Together. Through these events, our choir will sing several songs... we will entertain probably up to 40 or 50 other care homes.

Our performances extend beyond entertainment to service. We regularly appear at local churches to raise funds for various causes. This philanthropic dimension is deeply meaningful to choir members. The choir feels that they have such a nice life, and they're enjoying themselves so much that they want to give back to other people who don't have what they have.

One of our proudest achievements is our recording of You Raise Me Up, available on YouTube. A family member's grandson came and recorded us singing the song, and recorded a video for us as well. We even had a record launch event where Tim Howar from Mike and the Mechanics performed for us.

The local media have embraced our story, helping challenge stereotypes about dementia and showcasing what's possible when people are given opportunities rather than written off.

Each public appearance reinforces a crucial message to our choir members: they remain valued, capable members of society. We're not a bunch of people from a care home. We are a choir, I emphasise. This distinction is transformative shifting focus from what's been lost to what's being created.

These experiences beyond the care home have profound effects that linger. Residents discuss performances for days afterward, reliving favourite moments. Family members witness their loved ones in a new light, not as recipients of care but as contributors to community life.

I keep all the compliments we receive, written feedback from venues and audience members that I read to the residents. These affirmations matter enormously, validating the work we do and the joy we create.

The impact of these external performances extends beyond momentary pleasure. They forge new neural pathways, strengthen social bonds, and create a sense of anticipation that brightens everyday life. When residents know they'll be performing, it gives structure and purpose to their days.

For families, watching their loved ones perform can be profoundly moving. As one relative wrote after a concert. It was a moving experience to be part of something so special. I was moved to tears.

These comments capture what I see every time we perform the transformation that occurs when people with dementia are given opportunities to shine, to be seen not for what they've lost but for what they can create. In those moments on stage, dementia recedes into the background, and the person with all their talent and spirit steps forward into the light.

# CHAPTER 5: THE SCIENCE AND SPIRIT OF MUSIC

I stood in the hallway of the care home one morning, playing George Benson for a resident who struggles to speak clearly. As the music filled the corridor, something remarkable happened. His head is nodding, and he's clicking his fingers, he's trying to sing along with the lyrics. In that moment, I witnessed music reaching parts of the brain that nothing else could touch.

The numbers tell a sobering story about dementia in our society. Around 950,000 people in the UK alone have a diagnosis of dementia, estimated to reach one million by 2030. Worldwide, approximately 55 million people live with Alzheimer's. Behind these statistics are real people with rich histories and untapped potential. This is where music enters not just as entertainment, but as medicine for the mind and soul.

Research increasingly supports what I've observed firsthand. A 2017 systematic review found something striking. Among sensory stimulation interventions, the only convincingly effective intervention for reducing behavioral symptoms, specifically agitation, was music therapy.

Studies show that autobiographically salient music songs that hold special meaning to a person, like their wedding song, can actually stimulate neural connectivity in ways that help maintain higher levels of functioning. The music doesn't just evoke emotions, it creates pathways in the brain that medications simply cannot.

The effects are measurable. In a 2016 study of music therapy choirs, researchers found quality of life scores improved by 57 percent, while depressive symptoms were reduced by 54 percent. Even the World Health Organisation has recognised music's benefits for people with dementia, noting evidence for reducing anxiety and depression, supporting cognition, speech, and memory, reducing the need for antipsychotic drugs, and fewer and shorter stays in hospital.

But statistics and studies don't capture the magic I witness daily. Music therapy triggers the release of dopamine, the feel-good hormone. It boosts cognitive function, relieves symptoms of anxiety and stress, and helps with focus and memory. It activates various brain regions simultaneously, providing what researchers call a total brain workout.

One morning, I watched a resident who barely communicates verbally respond to Irish music. All of a sudden, he's up out of his chair. And we're doing an Irish jig around the lounge, and he's living his best life. For those moments, he wasn't a man with dementia; he was simply an Irishman dancing to beloved tunes from his homeland.

What continues to astonish me is that residents with dementia can learn completely new songs. We've been learning Perfect by Ed Sheeran. They might not remember every single word of it, but they remember most of it, particularly enjoying the chorus. This challenges common assumptions about dementia that learning new information is impossible.

Music also provides physical benefits. When we sing, we exercise our lungs and breathing. Singing provides this exercise naturally, without feeling like work.

Perhaps most profound is music's ability to create in-the-moment experiences. Dementia often leaves people disconnected from the present, caught between fading memories and confusion. Music anchors them firmly in the now. This distinction between feelings and memories revolutionised my understanding of dementia care. They don't remember exactly what I do, but I present them with a feeling. It's a feeling that something good is gonna happen.

Music creates a bridge not just between residents and staff, but between residents and their families, offering connection when words fail. Sometimes people say they think that their mum is gone, I say, emotion creeping into my voice, they can have that communication through music just for the hour, where their relative is there.

I've also observed how music can temporarily alleviate physical discomfort. As one resident shared, "I suffer with pains in my hands. And when I'm in the choir, I forget about it for a little while". This temporary relief from chronic pain is a precious gift.

Music fosters equality and community. Another resident noted, "When we are in the room at choir, we are all equal no matter what our problems". This leveling effect creates a rare space of dignity and belonging.

The social dimension of music therapy cannot be overstated. The World Health Organisation recognises music's socialising and bonding powers as invaluable as an invaluable antidote to isolation. In our choir, residents who previously isolated themselves have gradually emerged, drawn by the sounds of rehearsals and the community forming around them.

I've come to understand that music's power lies in how it accesses memories not through cognitive pathways but through emotional ones. Songs become embedded in our emotional memory in a way that makes them remarkably resilient to dementia's progression.

When we listen to music, we are in the moment, reliving a life and recalling happy memories. Music reaches more parts of the brain than anything else. It records our emotions. And by listening to music, it can reach people that we may think are unreachable.

I witnessed this truth one day with a resident who rarely communicates. I played his favorite Bob Marley song, and suddenly he was singing, jamming, jamming. For ten minutes, he was fully present, connected, joyful.

In these moments, I see not just the science of music therapy but its spirit, its capacity to restore personhood, dignity, and joy. The research confirms what our hearts already know: within each person with dementia, there remains a self that music can reach when nothing else can.

Unlike medications, music has no side effects except joy. Unlike many therapies, it requires no special equipment or clinical setting. It's accessible, affordable, and profoundly effective.

In the complex landscape of dementia care, music offers something precious: a path back to connection, to self-expression, to joy. Even when memory fades, music remembers us. It holds our stories, our emotions, our connections when we can no longer. Like a faithful friend, it stays beside us through the journey of dementia, reminding us of who we are, who we've been, and that we still belong.

# CHAPTER 6: STORIES OF TRANSFORMATION

Behind every choir session lie stories of transformation so profound they occasionally bring me to tears. These aren't dramatic Hollywood-style revelations, but quiet metamorphoses that change how residents experience themselves and their world.

The story that perhaps best captures our choir's impact began with a gentleman who positioned himself firmly by the door during our early sessions, close enough to observe but maintaining his boundary. He was sitting at the door, then he was in the middle of the room, and all of a sudden, he was in amongst the choir.

This gentle inch-by-inch approach yielded remarkable results. Not only did he eventually join us, but we went on to do shows with him, and he was like the star of the show. When his family visited, everything changed. He used to sing to the grandchildren and daughter-in-law because all of a sudden, he was part of a choir.

He developed a signature opera kind of voice that became his trademark. During one Christmas show, in the midst of a carefully rehearsed song, he stood up, and he started singing, and the whole audience was in stitches... they all started clapping, and he was taking a bow. His family could not believe the difference in him from withdrawn to expressive and confident, finding a new identity that transcended his diagnosis.

Another transformation began with a resident so excited about joining our choir that she immediately started writing out all the lyrics she could remember to her favourite song. Her enthusiasm shaped our entire approach to the choir, inspiring our use of lyric sheets and highlighting the power of engagement.

We have a lady who knows every word to every song. Her musical memory remains untouched by dementia, a phenomenon that continues to astonish me. She sings everything. She knows every single word. In her own words: "Music is everything to me. It's my favorite thing to do. So being in the choir is perfect for me".

For some residents, the choir provides structure and anticipation: "The choir gives me something to focus on. When I know choir practice is coming up, I feel excited and I look forward to it. Every day, I do ordinary things, but the choir is so different for me".

Others reconnect with earlier parts of their lives. "I used to sing when I was at school. I was in the school choir. When I came to the care home, I was so pleased they had a choir, so I joined immediately". This continuity is a precious thread of identity that dementia cannot sever.

The choir addresses emotional and social needs. "Being in the choir helps me socially, and I find it's a release when I can just sing out loud. When we all sing together, I feel that we are bonding". This sense of belonging creates connections that extend beyond choir sessions themselves.

Some discover that music offers temporary relief from physical discomfort. "I find that being in the choir helps me forget all my problems, aches, and pains for a while". This momentary reprieve from chronic pain is invaluable.

Perhaps most powerfully, residents find that the choir creates a space of equality. "I feel that when we are in the room at choir, we are all equal, no matter what our problems". In a world that often defines people by their limitations, this equality is revolutionary.

For some, the choir has built confidence. "I would never have spoken to strangers, never mind singing in front of them. But now I like to sit up the front and show off my talent". This newfound confidence often extends into everyday interactions.

Not everyone participates in the same way. We have one lady who doesn't sing at all; she has her baby, and she taps the baby. So she's tapping the baby, and her little feet are going. This individualised approach, honouring each person's unique way of engaging with music, is essential to our success.

Spontaneous musical moments often emerge outside formal sessions. One morning, residents spotted a dog outside and suddenly began singing "How Much Is That Doggy in the Window." Within moments, the whole room's singing... And then we're all laughing. These unplanned moments show how deeply music has integrated into residents' ways of being.

I've been moved to tears witnessing these transformations. One day, playing "Itsy Bitsy Teeny Weeny Yellow Polka Dot Bikini" in the hallway, I watched a resident who rarely communicates dancing with her teddy bear. She was there.

She was in that song, in that moment, and she was dancing. For those precious minutes, dementia receded, leaving just a woman dancing to a song that brought her joy.

For families, watching their loved ones transform through music can be deeply emotional. One daughter shared, "The One Voice choir team is doing an amazing job in motivating the residents at the care home through song. I have seen so many positive changes in my mum, and I thank you for that". These moments of recognition, seeing a parent come alive through music, are precious beyond measure.

Our choir challenges countless stereotypes about what people with dementia can enjoy and learn. When we sing Bruno Mars or Ed Sheeran, visitors are often shocked. They're like, 'Holy moly, we were expecting Knees up Mother Brown. Our residents aren't limited to songs from their youth, they're open to new experiences, new rhythms, and new stories.

Each story of transformation contains its unique melody. Together, they illustrate a simple truth: music doesn't just reach people with dementia, it helps restore them to themselves and to those they love.

# CHAPTER 7: A LEGACY OF JOY

As I sit in the quiet of my office at the care home, surrounded by photographs, mementos, and the folder of testimonials I've collected over the years, I'm struck by how far we've come. Our choir is entering its seventh year, a milestone that seemed unimaginable when we first began with a handful of residents tentatively singing "Heart of My Heart."

Seven years. In the landscape of dementia care, that's a remarkable stretch of time. Residents have come and gone. Voices have joined our harmony and later fallen silent. But something endures, a legacy that extends far beyond the notes we've sung or the venues we've played.

This is going into our seventh year of the choir, I tell people with a mixture of pride and wonder, and I think that's why we are going into our seventh year of the choir, because it's not something that I can just drop. Music is there for me for good.

Recognition for our work has come in various forms, each one affirming the value of what we've created together. We won an award at the Essex Care Sector Awards, a moment of validation that brought tears to my eyes. We've been featured in the newspaper countless times and appeared on the radio several times, talking to people about how the music feels for us and how we receive the music.

These public acknowledgments matter not because we seek fame, but because they help spread awareness about the potential of music in dementia care. Each article, each radio appearance, each award represents an opportunity to challenge misconceptions and demonstrate what's possible when people with dementia are given opportunities rather than limitations.

Our connection with Music for Dementia marked a significant turning point in our journey. I discovered this organisation while watching Vicky McClure's program, My Dementia Choir, on television. I watched that program, and I cried my eyes out. And I thought, that's us. That was so familiar to me.

Recognising our shared mission, I reached out to Music for Dementia, beginning a relationship that would profoundly impact our choir. Through them, we received a £1,000 grant from the National Academy of Social Prescribing, administered by the Utley Foundation. We used this funding to purchase a new speaker, a Bluetooth speaker, and some new uniforms, practical investments that enhanced our performances.

This generous funding has made possible projects we could once only dream about, including this book you're reading now. When I asked myself what to do with such a significant grant, the answer was clear: document our journey, share our story, and inspire others. The residents want their story to be out there. The residents want their story to be told so it will inspire other people to do what we do.

Their motivation is beautiful in its simplicity. If they can do it, anybody can do it. They want others to experience how much fun, joy and laughter, and everything else that comes along with it. They want to share the gift they've received.

We've discussed having a book launch where residents can sign copies and chat to people about their experiences. I remain amazed by their enthusiasm. They want people to read our book, and they want people to be inspired by what they do.

Within our company, I've already begun sharing our model. I spoke to all 75 care homes about how to set up a choir or a singing group. The feedback was overwhelmingly positive, suggesting that our approach can be replicated across many settings.

This ripple effect represents one of the most meaningful aspects of our legacy. By demonstrating what's possible even with limited resources and no formal musical training, we hope to inspire a movement of musical engagement in dementia care.

I hope that music is going to be more accessible for people with dementia in the future. Organisations like the Alzheimer's Society already offer Singing for the Brain groups, but we need more accessibility, more variety, more recognition of music's power.

In August 2024, we celebrated six years of the One Voice Choir with a party at the local church hall. Some might wonder why we marked six years rather than waiting for a more traditional milestone like five or ten. Our answer is simple and profound: In the care world, you do things as quickly as you can, as often as you and because you can. So we'll have a party, and people say, 'Oh, what's the party for?' Because we can. We don't have time to waste.

This awareness of time's preciousness infuses everything we do. The lineup of my choir changes all the time. But we have no time to waste. So we just make the most of every day, and we do things because we can.

Our choir has evolved from a simple activity into a vehicle for broader community engagement. Through performances and fundraising efforts, we've enabled residents to give back to causes they care about. Through the choir, the residents feel like they want to give back to the community. So we do a lot of things to raise money, to give back to people who are less fortunate than ourselves.

This aspect of our work addresses a fundamental human need that doesn't disappear with a dementia diagnosis: the desire to contribute, to help others, to make a difference. It makes them feel powerful. It makes them feel part of the community that they still have something to offer, that they can still give back to people.

One resident explained this feeling perfectly. We're using the talent that we have developed over the last seven years. We're using that for good. We're using that so we can give something back, and they love that because who doesn't wanna give back?

This sense of purpose transforms how residents see themselves and how others perceive them. They are productive members of the community. Not patients to be cared for, not burdens to be managed, but contributors with value to offer.

Perhaps the most profound aspect of our legacy is the transformation in how we understand dementia itself. It's a stage. It's the next stage of your life. It is not sad, doom and gloom, this is the end. It's a different stage of your life.

Through music, we've demonstrated that this stage can include joy, creativity, learning, and connection. For us, through music, we've been able to enhance that stage and go out performing, being on the radio, and singing for Tony Christie.

We've shown that people with dementia can learn new skills, adapt to new challenges, and experience genuine growth even in their 80s and 90s. They've just developed this whole new talent at 90 years old. How amazing is that? This challenges fundamental assumptions about aging and cognitive impairment.

Our choir has created a space where residents' identities extend beyond their diagnosis. When we get together as a choir, we're not a bunch of people from a care home. We are a working choir. This shift in perspective is revolutionary, focusing on what people can do rather than what they cannot.

For families, the choir offers a new way to connect with loved ones who might seem unreachable. One of the most moving aspects of our legacy is witnessing these reconnections. Sometimes people would think that their mom is gone, but they can have that communication just for an hour, where their mom is there, creating special memories.

These moments of connection, however temporary, provide precious respite from the grief that often accompanies dementia. They offer families glimpses of the person they love, reminders that beneath the confusion and memory loss, that person still exists.

The relationships formed through our choir often transcend traditional boundaries. We have family members who continue to volunteer with us even after their loved ones have passed, wanting to still make a difference. Relying on our amazing staff members' continuous support, we make this all possible.

This ongoing involvement speaks to the community we've created, one that extends beyond the care home walls to embrace families, volunteers, and supporters. It's a legacy of connection that outlasts individual members.

Each year brings new challenges and opportunities as our choir evolves. We adapt our repertoire to accommodate changing preferences and abilities. As we're going on, times are changing in the world, aren't they? And you're getting new members who are different ages. So the choir is changing.

This flexibility is essential to our continuing success. You can't just say, right, this is the formula, and we're gonna stick to that formula. The formula changes. You change. The residents change. Music is changing. How we access music is changing. You have to evolve with it, and that's what we are proudly doing.

As we look to the future, our ambitions remain both simple and profound. We want to keep doing our concerts. We want to keep doing our charity work, entertaining people, bringing happiness to people, and ourselves, and just inviting anybody who wants to come and have a look at our choir to come and join in.

We want to continue challenging stereotypes about what people with dementia can achieve. When we sing Elton John, visitors are often shocked. "Holy moly. We were expecting Daisy Daisy, they say, confronted with their own preconceptions about older people and music.

Most importantly, we want to inspire others to create their own musical communities. This book is part of that mission, an invitation and a roadmap for those who might think, I couldn't possibly do that. Our message is clear: if we can do it, so can you.

I often tell people, Everybody needs a Catherine. It's said with humor, but beneath the joke lies a deeper truth: every care setting needs someone passionate enough to push boundaries, to try new approaches, to believe in possibilities rather than limitations.

But here's the secret I've learned over these seven years: it's not about me. It's about creating spaces where people with dementia can reconnect with themselves and others through music. It's about recognising that even when memory fades, the capacity for joy remains intact. It's about understanding that music reaches more parts of the brain than anything else. Music that means something that is familiar correlates with memory and feeling.

The legacy we're creating isn't measured in awards or performances, though these have their place. It's measured in moments: the resident dancing in the hallway, the gentleman who surprises everyone with his opera voice, the family member who sees their mother truly present and engaged for the first time in months.

It's measured in the confidence of a resident who once refused to participate but now proudly declares: I would never have spoken to strangers, never mind singing in front of them. But now I like to sit up front and show off my talent.

It's measured in the sense of equality expressed by another resident. I feel that when we are in the room at choir room, we are all equal, no matter what our problems.

It's measured in moments of pure spontaneous joy, like when residents spotted a dog outside the window and the entire room burst into song, creating a moment of shared delight that brightened everyone's day.

As we enter our seventh year, I'm filled with gratitude for all we've experienced together and excitement for all that lies ahead. Our journey has taught me that music isn't just a pleasant diversion for people with dementia; it's a vital lifeline to self, to others, to joy. It doesn't just enhance life in many ways, it restores it.

In the end, perhaps our greatest legacy is simply this-proving that life with dementia can still be a life filled with purpose, connection, and joy. That a diagnosis isn't an ending but a different kind of beginning. That music can reach places that we may think are unreachable, bridging gaps, to touch the essentially human core that remains intact, waiting to be invited back into harmony.

*StoryTerrace*

Printed in Dunstable, United Kingdom